The Fun Run

by Zoë Clarke

illustrated by Janet Cheeseman

OXFORD
UNIVERSITY PRESS

Queen Max was on a fun run.

The queen was quick.

It was raining.
Fat toads sat in the path.

Queen Max put them back in the moat.

A big log fell.

Mud was on the path.
The mud was deep and wet.

The path had lots of thick weeds.
It was not fun!

I see big rocks on the path!

Queen Max did not win.

toads

log

mud

rocks

weeds

 Encourage the child to use the picture to retell the story.